Poppy!©2024
Written by Toby Glover
Illustrated by Jes Vazquez

enjoy
Toby

PAWESOME
PUBLISHING

A superhero!!!

...and fly to the sun!

...in the sky so blue!

I'll skipper a boat!

A cowboy outlaw!

Beep! Beep!

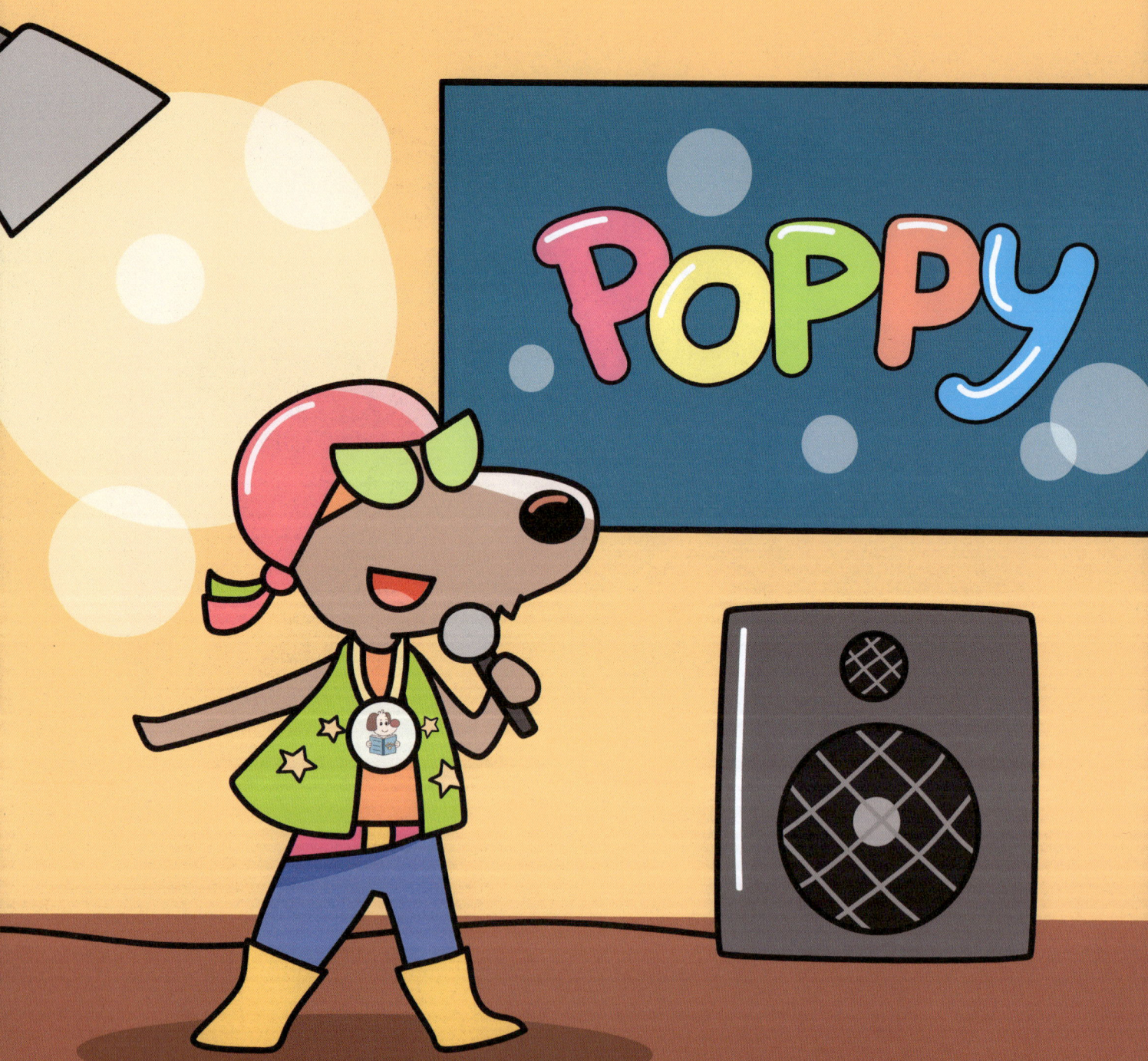

all the hits!

again

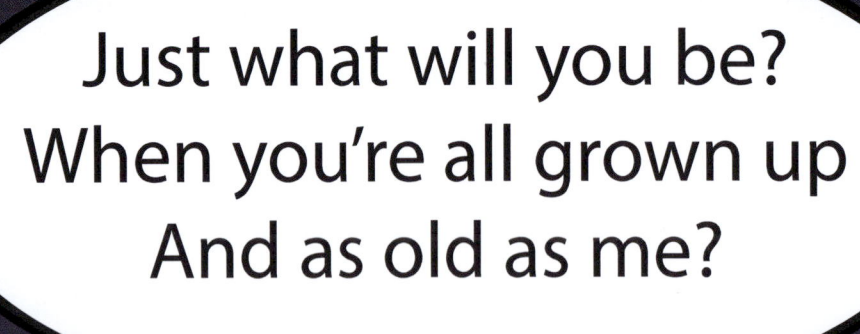

Favourite breed: Border terrier

Favourite food: Digestive biscuits

Favourite place: The woods

Favourite hobby: Foraging

Favourite human: Max

100% of all Pawesome Publishing profits are donated to animal charities.

Poppy has chosen *Tendercare Cat and Dog Rescue.*
They help homeless animals find happy homes, just like Poppy.
To find out more about this lovely charity, scan the QR code:

Thank you for being... PAWESOME!

PAWESOME PUBLISHING

To hear more of Toby's stories scan the QR

Printed in Great Britain
by Amazon